AWESOME ACTIVITIES

MARVELOUS MAGIC

Susan Martineau

Illustrations by Martin Ursell

WINDMILL
BOOKS™

New York

Published in 2012 by Windmill Books, LLC
303 Park Avenue South, Suite #1280, New York, NY 10010-3657

Adaptations to North American Edition © 2012 Windmill Books, LLC
© 2012 b small publishing ltd

Library of Congress Cataloging-in-Publication Data

Martineau, Susan.
Marvelous magic / by Susan Martineau. — 1st ed.
    p. cm. — (Awesome activities)
Includes index.
ISBN 978-1-61533-368-4 (library binding) — ISBN 978-1-61533-407-0 (pbk.) — ISBN 978-1-61533-468-1 (6-pack)
1. Magic tricks—Juvenile literature. I. Title.
GV1548.M373 2012
793.8—dc22
                                            2010052116

Manufactured in the United States of America

CPSIA Compliance Information: Batch #BS2011WM: For Further Information contact Windmill Books, New York, New York at 1-866-478-0556

Contents

You will need a bit of grown-up help in one or two places. These have been marked with this special symbol. !

Before You Begin

You'll probably already have most of the things you need for these tricks and costumes around the house. For great disguises, you could start collecting old jackets, glasses and sunglasses, hats, scarves, and so on. Yard sales and thrift shops are great places to find things, too.

Be sure to practice your tricks before doing them for your friends and family. Choose one of the special disguises to wear in your act. When you are ready to perform, remember that you don't want your **audience** too close. It's also best not to play the practical jokes on anyone who gets upset easily!

Magic Banana Trick

Prepare this wacky trick and leave it in a fruit bowl. When someone wants a banana, make sure to offer them this one!

What you will need:
- 1 banana
- A toothpick

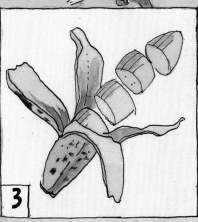

1 Push the toothpick into the banana carefully. Move it slowly from side to side, so that it slices the banana inside.

2 Repeat this a few times along the banana. The holes will look like speckles on the skin.

3 When it's peeled, just watch your friends' faces.

Magic Circles

The International Brotherhood of Magicians is the largest magic society in the world. It has nearly 15,000 members. The society is based in St. Charles, Missouri. It was founded in 1922. It also has a junior section called Magical Youth International. It's a great club to join if you're crazy about magic!

Matchbox Magic

Cool Coin Trick

You'll really confuse your friends and family with this nifty trick. You'll need to be wearing a long-sleeved shirt or sweatshirt to perform it.

What you will need:
- 4 identical empty matchboxes
- Some coins
- Tape

1 Place the coins in one matchbox. Push it up your right sleeve so that it will be out of sight. Tape it to your wrist.

2 Place the other three empty boxes on the table. Ask your friends to gather around.

3 Using your left hand, pick up a box and shake it. Then pick up and shake a second box. They will both sound empty.

Fastest Wand in the World

The fastest magician in the world is Eldon D. Wigton, also known as Dr. Eldoonie. On April 21, 1991 he performed 225 different tricks in two minutes!

"clink"

4

Pick up the third box with your right hand and shake it. The coins up your sleeve will rattle. Move the boxes around. Only move them using your left hand! See if anyone can guess which one has the coins in it.

6

The Moving Matchbox

This is a simple but rather creepy trick. At your command, the matchbox on the back of your hand will stand up!

What you will need:
- An empty matchbox

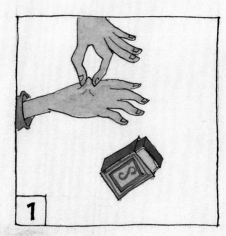

1

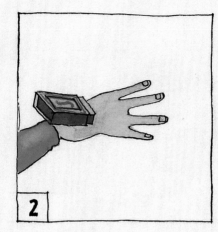

2

3

Pull the drawer of the matchbox a little way out. Squeeze the skin on the back of your hand.

Catch the skin between the drawer and the outer box. Close the drawer carefully to keep the skin trapped.

Keep your wrist straight and your hand open. The box will lie flat. Bend your wrist and close your hand. The box will stand up.

The Disappearing Magician

In 1939, William "Doc" Nixon disappeared without a trace. This magician, who liked to appear in a costume, was never seen again!

POP!

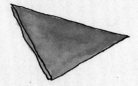

BANG!

Slap in the Face!

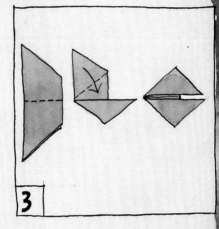

This trick has probably been a favorite since paper was invented. Have a trusting friend help you with this one.

What you will need:
• A sheet of letter size paper

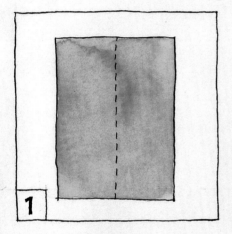

1

Fold the paper in half, lengthwise. Open it up again.

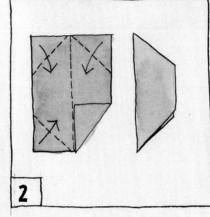

2

Fold in each corner to meet the fold in the middle. Fold the paper in half.

3

Make a crease in the middle. Fold both points down so that the long edges meet the middle crease.

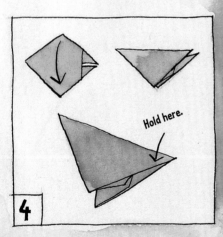

Hold here.

4

Turn the paper over. Fold the two points together.

Now you are ready for action! Hold the folded paper by its bottom points and whoosh it down quickly. At the same time pretend to slap your friend! It makes a great sound effect!

BANG!

Predictatrick

This is lots of fun and will **mystify** your friends. You need to be facing your audience.

What you will need:
- Pencil or pen
- 8 small sheets of paper
- A hat or bag

1

Ask your friends to call out eight different numbers.

2

Make sure they cannot see what you are writing. Write only the first number that was called out on EVERY sheet.

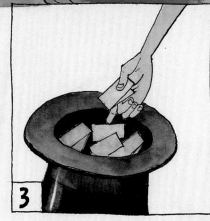

3

Fold the sheets and place them in the hat or bag. Ask a friend to pick one. Then tell everyone what is written on the sheet. They will be amazed when they open it to check!

Spooky Prediction

In 1898, fourteen years before the sinking of the *Titanic*, a book called *The Wreck of the Titan* was published. It was the story of a vast ocean liner that hits an iceberg. Was the author, a man named Morgan Robertson, able to see into the future or was this just an eerie **coincidence**?

9

Make a Magic Wand

It's really easy to make your own magic wand. You can use it for all your tricks, including the one here!

What you will need:
- 6-inch (16 cm) long wooden stick
- Pencil
- Masking tape

- Black paint and white paint
- Paintbrush
- Clay

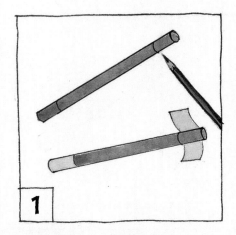

1

Make pencil marks 1 inch (2 cm) in from the ends of the stick. Wrap masking tape around the ends.

2

Paint the main part of the stick black. When it's dry, remove the tape.

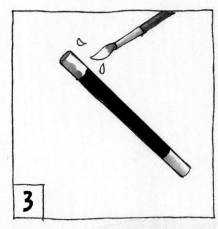

3

Paint the ends white and let them dry.

Magic Tip

Use the clay to hold the wand steady as you paint it.

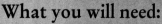

Aargh, My Leg!

This is a simple, but scary, trick! You might want to practice this in front of a mirror before your performance.

What you will need:
- Thick white paper
- Scissors
- Your magic wand
- Glue

1

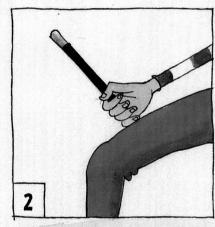

2

3

Cut a piece of paper one inch (2 cm) wide. Roll it into a tube to fit round the wand. Glue the edge carefully.

Hold the wand as shown. Hide the end on your leg with one hand.

With the other hand, gradually push the tube down the wand. Keep the end of the wand hidden behind your hand and wrist. Ouch!

The Legless Trickster

Eliaser Bamberg was a court magician in eighteenth-century Holland. He lost a leg in an accident and had a special **artificial** one made with all kinds of compartments. He could perform amazing tricks using this "magical" limb!

All Tied Up

The Great Knot Challenge

Challenge your friends to tie a simple knot in a short piece of rope without letting go of the ends at all! Then show them how it's done.

What you will need:
- A piece of string or rope about 50 inches (127 cm) long

1 Place the rope or string in front of you. Fold your arms completely.

2 Pick up one end of the rope or string in each hand.

3 Unfold your arms and you've tied a knot! It's easy when you know how.

Pull a Rope Through Your Neck!

You know you should never put ropes around your neck.
You don't in this trick, but it looks like you do.

What you will need:

- A piece of rope about 50 inches (127 cm) long
- A turtleneck sweater or shirt

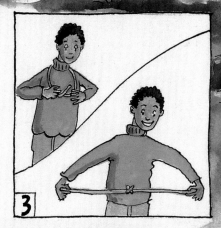

1 Hold the rope in the middle. Then tuck the middle part under the front of the turtleneck.

2 The two ends should hang down in front of you. It now looks like the rope is around your neck. Of course, it isn't really!

3 Gather your audience. Tie the ends of the rope in a knot at your neck. Yank it fast and pull the rope away from you.

The Great Escape

Harry Houdini is one of the most famous magicians and escape artists ever. Audiences would suggest impossible places to escape from and Harry would do it! He could escape from padlocked crates thrown into rivers, giant paper bags without tearing them, and even a bronze coffin submerged in a swimming pool.
He died on Halloween in 1926—spooky!

Sick Snacks

Offer your friends a delightful snack! This is great for Halloween parties or any dark and spooky night.

Eyeballs on the Rocks

Make these gory ice cubes the night before you want to use them.

What you will need:

- Large radishes
- Small black olives, stoned
- Sharp knife
- Ice-cube tray
- Big can of tomato juice

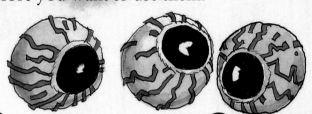

1

Peel the radishes, leaving a bit of red skin on them.

2

With the tip of the knife, dig a small hole in each radish. Push an olive into each hole.

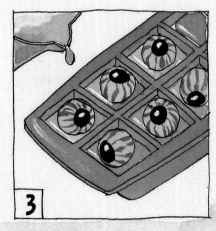

3

Pop the stuffed radishes into the slots of the tray. Fill the tray with water and let it freeze overnight.

4

Fill some glasses with tomato juice and pop a couple of eyeballs in each!

Toasted Tongues

What you will need to serve 2 people:

- 4 slices of bread
- 2 slices of salami or ham
- Scissors and a knife
- Cutting board
- Toaster oven
- Ketchup

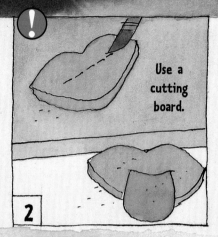

Use a cutting board.

1

2

3

Cut each slice of bread into a mouth shape using scissors. Cut four tongues out of the ham or salami.

Cut a slit between the lips using the knife. Pop a tongue into each mouth.

Place the mouths in the toaster oven and toast lightly. Serve with the ketchup.

Vampires!

Stories about vampires have been around since Roman times. All over the world, you can find legends about beings that drink human blood in order to live forever. There's a Chinese vampire with red eyes and green hair, a Malaysian one that trails its insides along behind it, and a Greek creature that is half woman, half snake.

The most famous vampire of all is Count Dracula from the book by Bram Stoker. The author based his character on a real-life count from Transylvania. The count was known as Vlad the Impaler because of the bloodthirsty way in which he got rid of people he didn't like!

Icky Zits and Beastly Boils

Yuck! Yuck! Yuck! These delightful zits and boils can be applied anywhere on your body. Make them as big as you like and experiment with different colors. Yellow and green are perfect for pus! Why not combine some with the bald head on page 22 for a really disgusting disguise?

What you will need:
- Washable markers
- Tissues
- Liquid glue
- Paintbrush

Tear off small bits of tissue. Use the markers to color them yellow, red, brown, or green. You can mix colors, too.

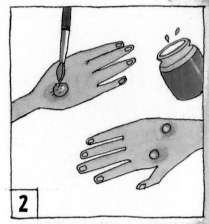

Scrunch up the tissue bits and place them on your skin. Brush some glue all over and around them. Let them dry.

Revolting Warts

Paint some latex, or art masking fluid, thickly on to a flat plastic lid. Let it dry and then roll it up as you peel it off the lid.

Black Death Buboes

During the fourteenth century, millions of people were wiped out by a disease called the Black Death. Not only did your skin turn black but you also got gross lumps called buboes in your armpit and other parts of your body.

Color the dried latex or masking fluid with markers. Glue it to your skin.

Mega-sneeze Wheeze

This trick is a gross but really simple joke. It produces rather surprising results, especially if you make a bit of trick snot to go with it.

What you will need:
- A small handkerchief or tissue
- A very bouncy rubber ball
- A rubber band

Trick Snot

To make latex snot, see the warts on page 16. Color it green. Curl it into a ball and hold it close to your nose as you "sneeze." Watch your friends' faces as you unroll the "snot" from your nose!

1

2

3

Place the ball in the center of the hanky or tissue. Gather the hanky or tissue around it and put the rubber band around it tightly.

Put it all in your pocket and wait for a "sneeze" to come along.

How does he do it?

Hold the hanky or tissue in both hands with the ball inside. As you "sneeze" throw the whole thing on the ground in front of you.

The Bullet Catch

Many magicians have died in the attempt to perform this most dangerous of tricks, catching a bullet fired from a gun in their teeth or on a plate.

Most mysterious was the death of Chung Ling Soo in 1918. He died after trying the Bullet Catch. After his death, it turned out he was not Chinese at all. He was an American called William E. Robinson.

Headless Horror

You'll need a friend to help you with this horrible practical joke. You also need to be wearing a pair of pants or a skirt that you can hitch up under your armpits. Please remember not to frighten your granny!

What you will need:
- Large piece of cardboard
- Scissors
- Tape
- Large piece of red fabric, such as an old T-shirt or towel
- Very large shirt
- Large, adult-sized jacket

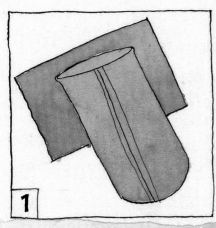

1 Curl the cardboard into a tube and tape it firmly.

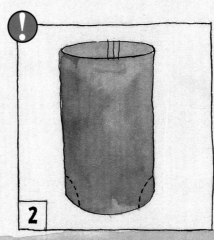

2 Cut the tube as shown. It should sit well on your shoulders.

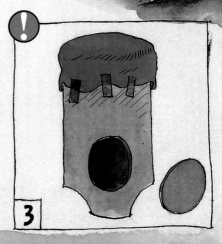

3 Cut a hole for your head. Cover the top end with the fabric and tape it firmly.

The Headless Horseman

Beware the Dullahan! In Irish legend, he is a terrifying headless horseman who rides an awful black steed. He holds his head under his arm, the huge eyes staring. His face looks like moldy cheese. If the Dullahan knocks on your door, he'll throw a bucket of blood at you. The only thing he is afraid of is gold. You can save yourself from certain death with a gold ring.

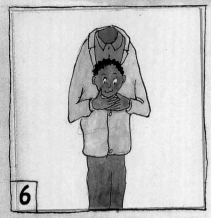

4 Hitch your trousers or skirt up. Get your friend to dress you in the shirt. Button it up around your head! Tuck it in.

5 Put the jacket on over the shirt. Put your arms through the sleeves. Do up the bottom of the jacket.

6 Hold your head in your hands and go in search of your first victim!

The Headless Earl

Thomas Percy, seventh Earl of Northumberland, was executed for treason by Elizabeth I of England. His head was put on a spike and his body was buried. It is said that the ghost of the Headless Earl can be seen stumbling about in search of his severed head!

Terrible Tips

You could paint your face white and gel your hair. Make a set of vampire fangs out of a piece of a white plastic yogurt cup.

Old Before Your Years

Even your mother may not recognize you like this! The hideous headgear on page 22 looks really great with this disguise. Why not add the mustache, too?

The Anti-Facelift

Screw up your eyes and see where the wrinkles appear. Open your eyes and use an eyebrow pencil to draw along each crease. You'll age by decades!

Draw creases and wrinkles around your mouth and nose.

Draw bags under your eyes with the pencil, too. Shade underneath for amazingly aged eyes. Make your eyebrows look shaggier by pencilling in some more bushy bits.

Half wolf, half man!

An old, old **superstition** says that there are certain people who can change into frightening wolves. Scientists have looked into this belief and think there may really be an illness that can make people hairy and violent!

Change Your Shape

Wear your normal clothes. Start adding padding on top of them.

1 Tie cushions round your waist using string or rope.

4 On top, wear clothes that are a few sizes too big. Wear big shoes, too.

2 Wind scarves and small towels around your arms and legs.

5 Practice walking in a stooped way. Maybe add a cane to finish the disguise.

3 Put a towel around your shoulders.

The Shape of Fashion

Strange and amazing shapes have often been the fashion. In sixteenth-century Spain, it was really cool for men to pad the front of their jackets with a false potbelly! The extra stuffing was made from bits of wool or horsehair.

During the reign of Elizabeth I of England, the fashion for women included a farthingale. This was a fat roll of cushioning worn around the hips to make dresses stick out. It was meant to show off the **embroidery** on the material.

Devious Disguises

Where's Your Hair?

Try and get your hands on some old, unwanted make-up for this. You could also make this with cotton balls.

What you will need:
- Newspaper
- Old white rubber swimming cap
- Pencil
- 6-inch (14 cm) by 1-inch (3 cm) strip of cardboard
- Glue
- White or gray wool
- Scissors
- Eyebrow pencil
- Cream foundation

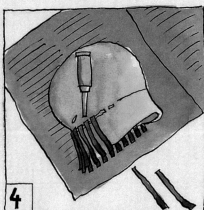

1 Cover your work surface with newspaper. Turn the cap inside out. Draw a line 2 inches (5 cm) up from the bottom.

2 Wind lots of wool around the cardboard. Cut the wool along one edge and lay out the strands.

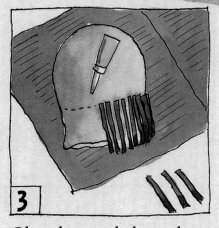

3 Glue the wool along the line on the cap. Leave a gap of 2 inches (5 cm) at one end. Let the cap dry.

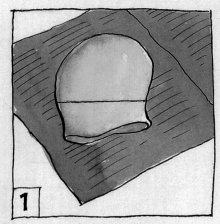

4 Turn the cap over and repeat. Don't forget to leave the 2-inch (5 cm) gap. Let it dry again.

5 Pull the cap on. Cover the bald head with foundation to blend it in with your own skin.

6 Add wrinkles on the forehead using the eyebrow pencil. Trim the hair a bit if necessary.

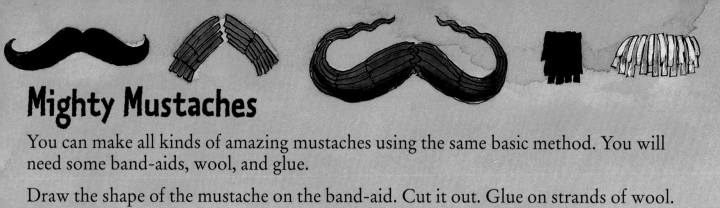

Mighty Mustaches

You can make all kinds of amazing mustaches using the same basic method. You will need some band-aids, wool, and glue.

Draw the shape of the mustache on the band-aid. Cut it out. Glue on strands of wool. Two layers looks good.

Peel the backing off the band-aid and press it against your face!

You could even make some bushy sideburns or eyebrows using the same technique. You'd be completely unrecognizable!

For a white mustache, use cotton balls. Tie a piece of thread in the center. Glue two small bits of band-aid to it before sticking it on your face.

Read More

Becker, Helaine. *Secret Agent Y.O.U.: The Official Guide to Secret Codes, Disguises, Surveillance, and More*. Toronto: Maple Tree Press, 2006.

Bree, Loris. *Kids' Magic Secrets: Simple Magic Tricks & Why They Work*. St. Paul, Minnesota: Marlor Press, 2003.

Cleeland, Holly. *Glue & Go Costumes for Kids: Super-Duper Designs with Everyday Materials*. New York: Sterling Books, 2006.

Glossary

artificial (ar-tih-FIH-shul) Made by people, not nature.

audience (AH-dee-ints) A group of people who watch or listen to something.

coincidence (KOH-ints-uh-dents) Things happening in the same way or at the same time by chance.

embroidery (em-BROY-deh-ree) Decoration with needlework.

mystify (mis-TUH-fy) To confuse.

superstition (soo-pur-STIH-shun) A belief that something is unlucky.

Index

Web Sites

For Web resources related to the subject of this book, go to: www.windmillbooks.com/weblinks and select this book's title.